# MORGAN
### *and the*
# Sock Thief

Written by
Mary C. Whitton

(Inspired by true events.)

Illustrations by Timothy Warren

Literary Division for Young Readers
THE KODEL GROUP, LLC
EMPIRE HOLDINGS

# Morgan and the Sock Thief

(Inspired by true events.)

Original Story Written by
Mary C. Whitton

Illustrations by Timothy Warren
Edited by Melissa Beggs
Proofreader Nancy Ellen Holt

First Edition

©
Copyright 2015
Worldwide Rights Reserved

New York   New Zealand   Hong Kong   Mexico City   Johannesburg
Tokyo   Toronto   Paris   Copenhagen   London   Sydney   Dublin   New Delhi

**Published by**
**The Kodel Group, LLC**
Imprint: Empire Holdings - Literary Division for Young Readers
P.O. Box 38, Grants Pass, Oregon, USA 97528
KodelEmpire.com  ✪  StevieTenderheart.com

Editor-in-Chief: Steve William Laible, MBA
Prepared for Publication by Vicky Rummel

Print ISBN 978-1-62485-007-3          eBook ISBN 978-1-62485-030-1

Printed in the United States of America, Europe, Asia and beyond...

# DEDICATION

To Bill Causley – the real Uncle Poppy and my rock in life.

To Harriet Herr, who gave us the gift of TC.

To my parents, Elliott and Iris Whitton who were the real people next door.

To Dr. Debi Watanabe for her loving and dedicated Veterinarian care of TC.

A *special thanks* to Brian Rono who originally inspired the writing of this book by *his* rescue of a senior dog from a shelter.  His name was DUKE.

*Mary C. Whitton*

# ACKNOWLEDGEMENTS

In loving memory of my brother,
Michael E.Whitton

To Kaylee Wong and Mary Casas,
for your encouragement, interest, and support...

# Morgan and the Sock Thief

*by* MARY C. WHITTON

***illustrations*** *by* Timothy Warren

# CONTENTS

Life has a way of
opening itself to
possibilities.
The unexpected...
leaving us
innocent and
oblivious
of what lies
around the bend.
Some people call
it destiny,
others call these
events miracles.

For Morgan...
just one
day later
might have
made all the
difference
in the world...
The unexpected
takes her along
the path
of discovery...

Mary C. Whitton

# Morgan and the Sock Thief

## A STORY OF LOVE AND RESCUE

## Mary C. Whitton

### INSPIRED BY A TRUE STORY

## Introduction

### *The Old Woman*

At eighty years old, she found it difficult to climb the few steps that led into the animal shelter. Her legs felt heavy, as if they had a mind of their own and refused to cross the threshold. She stood motionless in the open doorway, firmly gripping a small cage. Knowing her fate, she purposefully willed herself to move forward. Once inside, she sat down on a nearby bench to rest. The saddened woman needed a fresh dose of courage to continue. The guilt and helplessness she felt reminded her of no other time in her life. She was about to give up all that she loved, all she had left in the world.

A volunteer stepped forward to help the troubled lady.

The older woman tried to blink away her tears. The tightness in her throat made her voice crack.

"Promise me that you will protect my dog. Find a good home with people who will love her. This is all I ask."

The volunteer understood. It was her job to receive the animals in need. However, she never managed to escape the sadness.

3

The volunteer carefully lifted the crate from the woman's lap and tried to comfort her in a kindhearted tone. "I will personally watch over your dog and place her with a loving family as soon as possible. I give you my promise."

The heartbroken woman said goodbye to her beloved dog.

She looked back at her little friend one last time ... as she tearfully left the building.

# 1

# *Morgan*

The day came when Morgan knew she could no longer wait for the decision. She approached her father, who was working in his study, and said, "I want to know if it is true."

"True? If what is true, honey?" her father casually inquired.

"I want to know if you really meant it, when you said *someday* I could have a dog of my own. Last year, you thought I was too young. Now I am almost eleven! That's a good age. Don't you think, Dad?"

"Raising a puppy is not a good idea for us right now. We tell you this every time you ask," grumbled her father as he glanced up at her.

"I know," replied the determined girl, "but this time I am not asking for a puppy. What if we adopt an already grown dog?"

Her father pondered that idea for a moment and did not have an answer. Morgan knew her parents didn't want a puppy because there was no time for training. The persistent girl asked repeatedly. Morgan promised she would take good care of a pet.

Last year, she was almost certain a pup would be under the tree on Christmas morning. While she found many other gifts for which she was grateful, in her heart she was disappointed about not receiving a puppy. Morgan tried to be cheerful that Christmas. She smiled through the festive day and never told anyone about how she truly felt. Instead, she waited. Children wait. That's what they do, and she was no different.

Now, Morgan waited with new hope while her parents discussed the idea of adopting an already grown and trained dog.

Just then, she heard footsteps coming up the stairs. For one second, she allowed herself a leap of excitement, and then quickly shuddered to think those footsteps might also bring the bearer of the usual bad news.

"We've decided to take you to the animal shelter tomorrow. I suppose there's no harm in just *looking* at the adoptable dogs," her father said with a wink.

Her mom then entered the room. Morgan jumped up from her desk and hugged her around the waist. She looked up into her mother's face and didn't have to say anything. Unspoken words sometimes express everything.

Her father smiled and declared, "No guarantees, honey. We are just going to look. We will take all the time we need to make the right choice. Do you understand?"

"Yes, Dad, I do."

## 2

# *The Shelter*

When they entered the shelter, it suddenly occurred to Morgan that choosing a dog might be more difficult than she thought. However, this realization did not alter her excitement. She could hear an orchestra of muffled howling and woofing coming from a faraway part of the shelter.

A volunteer offered to guide them through the adoption process.

"We want to be sure that any animal we place goes to a warm and caring home," said the volunteer.

She asked Morgan and her parents a list of questions. Morgan thought she must have passed a test, because the volunteer then led them down a long passageway towards the kennels. The howling and yelping voices grew much louder and more intense, each with its own pitch and distinction.

They stepped beyond the steel gate, but once inside, Morgan stopped. Her eyes peered down the narrow corridor of cement runs and cages, her father by her side. The reality of the moment shocked Morgan. The scene before her was no longer just confined to her imagination. The metallic echoes, the sharp smell, the deafening competition of so much barking made the experience a little overwhelming.

She stood there, frozen ... taking it all in.

"Let's go through now, honey, and look at the dogs," urged her father.

Morgan walked slowly ahead, only occasionally kneeling in front of a cage. Many curious dogs sniffed her hand as she tried to pet them through the metal bars. She proceeded down the corridor. The volunteer gave a history of each dog and answered any questions.

Morgan viewed all the anxious faces of the homeless dogs that day, each with its own story. Some dogs were jumping up and down and smiling playfully.

A few dogs performed tricks as if to advertise their adoptability. Others remained quiet, looking the most sad and lonely. Mostly, all of them were waiting ... waiting to be chosen. Many of the dogs were too big, and Morgan knew better than to ask for one of the adorable puppies.

"You will know it when you see the right dog," said her mom. "Just look into their eyes. If you don't find one now, we can come back in a few days."

"But Mom, I want to take one home today! I know the right dog is here for me. He just has to be."

Just then, Morgan's father, who had gone ahead, called out to his wife and daughter.

"Girls, come here and look at this one."

Just behind the gate of a long, cement dog run sat a small wire cage with a tiny animal inside.

"Ah!" said the volunteer, "That is a special dog. She is a Teacup Poodle. It is rare to find a dog like this in a shelter," she continued.

Morgan knelt down to get a closer look. All she could

see were two tiny black eyes staring back at her. Pressed against the back corner of the cage was a little silver dog, cowering, shaking, and scared.

"A lady brought her in just yesterday," explained the volunteer.

"But why is she in that cage?" asked Morgan.

"This is how she was delivered to us. For now, she is more comfortable and secure in her own cage. It is all she knows."

"Why would someone want to give her away?" asked Morgan.

"The brave woman I met yesterday could no longer care for her," answered the volunteer. She told Morgan and her parents more about the elderly woman who had to give up the miniature dog.

"I have witnessed many sad moments here at the shelter, but this one was especially moving," said the volunteer.

Morgan did not fully grasp the whole story. Only a blurry image entered her mind of the lady who had to leave her caged pet behind at a shelter. She did not want to think about it now. She heard the adults discussing the details in the background, but she easily tuned them out, allowing her mind to wander as she imagined the possibilities.

"May I take her out and hold her?" asked Morgan.

The volunteer lifted her out. She put the dog carefully in Morgan's arms and said, "Her name is Teacup."

"Teacup," Morgan whispered as she looked up at her mother.

The volunteer continued, "Teacup is not a young dog, and she is very delicate, weighing only four pounds. She is already over ten years old and needs a home with people who can care for an aging dog. You must consider her age and determine if you can take on this kind of responsibility."

"Teacup only has a few more years left to live. Do you

understand?" the volunteer repeated, gently directing her words to Morgan.

"Yes," Morgan responded with a slow nod.

Morgan's parents asked the volunteer more questions while she held the fragile animal. The volunteer watched how Morgan handled the dog. The trembling poodle soon became still in Morgan's arms. Morgan felt as if she could never let go. The voices and loud noises of the shelter gradually faded into a silent moment. To Morgan, it felt as if she and Teacup were suspended in a time bubble that held just the two of them. She wanted to rescue this precious pet as much as Teacup wanted to stay cradled in Morgan's arms.

Morgan broke into the huddled adults' conversation and asked, "Can we adopt her?"

Just as her mother started to answer the question, the volunteer interrupted. "Each adoption must be evaluated by our staff and approved before we can let you take her home."

"Oh, please Mother, I *know* I can care for Teacup. I will give her the best home ever!" exclaimed Morgan intensely. "This is the dog I want. I think she belongs with *me* now."

Morgan turned towards the volunteer and promised to follow all the shelter rules. If given a chance, she desperately wanted to prove she could care for a special animal.

The volunteer smiled at the sincere girl and said kindly, "Let's put Teacup back in her cage for now and go to my office."

Morgan reluctantly complied and put the whimpering

poodle back into her little crate.

"Please be seated," said the volunteer. "Usually, we try to place the special dogs with older people. It is a guideline here, but let me speak to the Director. I'll see what I can do."

Morgan's parents signed the pending adoption papers while she waited quietly. She thought only of the helpless poodle behind the tall doors. *Teacup must be so lonely and scared.* If she passed the final approval, Morgan intended to give her new dog a perfect home.

Morgan's father spoke up on behalf of his daughter, "My girl is young and inexperienced with dogs, but she is a loving person and sensitive to the needs of others. If an exception could be made, I can honestly say you will not be sorry."

"Oh Daddy, you want to take her home too, don't you?"

"Yes, honey, I think I do."

"I will contact you as soon as I have an answer," replied the volunteer. "You will know our decision by this afternoon."

Back at home, the passing hours consumed Morgan with worry. Her mother tried to reassure her. Nevertheless, waiting was a familiar torture.

*Surely*, Morgan thought, *they must know. They must know that I belong with this dog.*

When the phone rang later that afternoon, Morgan's father took the call. His facial expressions revealed no clues. He just listened to the shelter volunteer as Morgan and her mother looked on.

He set the phone down and reported, "They will allow us to take Teacup home for one week on a trial basis. We will be foster parents. This way we can all see if it is a fitting match."

"Do I have to give her back after one week, Dad?"

He gave his daughter a sympathetic smile and replied, "No Morgs, we just need to return next weekend for a routine evaluation. Afterwards, she will be ours. That is, if we are happy with her, and if she is happy with us. Is this understood?"

"Oh, yes, but I know she will love us and want to stay forever! Can we go get her right now?"

"Yes," agreed her father, "Let's go right now."

Morgan's father carried their new pet out to the car. He placed the cage, with the dog in it, on the back seat. Morgan climbed in next to her.

Morgan's mother leafed through the box of items that came with the dog. It contained an old camera bag with a flat pillow at the bottom, a pink flannel blanket, and a tiny yellow raincoat. She also pulled out a stuffed rabbit with a missing eye and half-chewed ear, and one white sock.

"Can I take Teacup out and hold her, Dad?"

"No, honey, I think it is best if she stays in her familiar spot until we get home."

Morgan stroked the dog's fur through the fenced door of the cage. She could see that Teacup was afraid.

"You have to be gentle and slow moving until she adapts to her new home and a new family," cautioned her mother.

Morgan understood, but found it difficult to hold back her long-awaited excitement. She hungered for the day when Teacup would become her best friend.

Upon arriving home, Morgan's father carried the dog into the backyard. When the cage door opened, the frightened poodle studied the sunny garden but did not step out. Morgan reached in and lifted Teacup out, the same way she had seen the volunteer do it at the shelter. Morgan sat cross-legged on the lawn and put the liberated pet on her lap. Her parents coached her all the way. They advised Morgan to let the dog move on her own. With one tiny paw after another, the timid dog started to explore her new domain.

Mary C. Whitton

## 3

# *Life with Morgan*

Morgan and her family did everything possible to make Teacup feel welcomed. At first, Morgan wrapped her new dog in a warm blanket and carried her everywhere. She slowly and gently introduced Teacup to her new surroundings.

On the second and third day, Teacup followed Morgan everywhere like a gosling in single file behind a mother goose. Teacup never let Morgan out of her sight.

The weekend passed. Monday was a school day for Morgan. She begged her mom to let her stay home. Morgan claimed that Teacup needed her more than ever right now.

"She is only happy with me. I really think I should skip school today," whined Morgan.

"I know she loves you the best," replied her mother. "This is great, sweetie, but she also needs to be content with daddy and me too, when you are away or doing other things. She will be glad to see you when you get home. Your school work and piano practice must not suffer from this, or we will have problems, right?"

"Yes, Mom, but remember, she needs you to pet her sometimes, and don't do anything to frighten her," instructed Morgan.

Her mother smiled and told her not to worry. "Everything will be fine. Just focus on doing well in school."

Morgan and her mom walked down the street to the corner. Teacup trotted alongside on the leash. Morgan boarded the school bus and chose a seat by the window. Her mom held Teacup and gave Morgan a wave with Teacup's paw. Morgan waved back as the bus pulled away. She believed that Teacup had a worried look on her face.

Later, on the bus ride home from school, Morgan was excited because her English teacher gave the class an interesting assignment. He instructed them to write a poem about an important event in their lives. Morgan knew the exact topic for her poem.

When Morgan arrived home, she was thrilled to see Teacup. It was the first time they had been separated in three days. Teacup scampered across the carpet to Morgan. She balanced on her hind legs like a circus dog, raising her front paws, wanting to be picked up. Already, a trust existed between the two of them. Morgan thought it was because the dog sensed, in some way, that Morgan had rescued her.

Morgan rolled around on the living room floor to play with Teacup. Immediately, Teacup pounced on her stuffed rabbit with the missing eye and half-chewed ear ... the only toy brought from her previous life. She snatched it and ran, so Morgan could not get it first. Morgan attempted to take the rabbit from Teacup. It became obvious that this was not a two-way game. Teacup pretended to give Morgan a chance at the rabbit. She froze in place, daring Morgan to come closer. She then launched into a game of hide and seek, darting in and out of spaces between the furniture that were too small for Morgan. It was Teacup's moment to shine. The living room carpet was her stage and cuteness was her role.

Morgan and her mother sat back and watched Teacup's solo performance. It amused them to watch her toss the rabbit up in the air, then tackle it, then toss again. In between tosses, she clenched the stained rabbit in her mouth and pranced about like a proud show pony, welcoming applause from her fans.

Teacup appeared to be secure and happy with her new family. However, at times, she seemed confused and unsettled, whimpering unexpectedly. Teacup would suddenly raise her head up, tilting it to one side. She would perk up her ears and stare at the door, as if she heard the startling sound of a dog whistle not audible to humans ... or perhaps she heard a distant voice calling her from a remembered past.

Morgan walked upstairs to her bedroom. Following close behind, Teacup hopped from step to step, pushing off with her back paws like a bunny.

Once in her bedroom, Morgan laid Teacup on the flannel blanket left by the old woman that fateful day at the shelter. Something curious about that worn pink flannel from Teacup's past always made her circle round and round, then curl up into a tight ball every time Morgan placed her on it.

Morgan sat on the bed next to her pampered pet. She was eager to finish the assigned homework that she had started on the bus. Teacup snoozed while Morgan continued writing her poem. Later, she carried the sleepy poodle into the family room, where her parents usually relaxed after dinner.

"You've been quiet upstairs all evening. Are you and the 'little one' doing all right?" asked her mom.

"Yes, Mom, I was working on my poem. I wrote about 'you know who.' Do you want to hear what I wrote?"

"Yes, honey, we would love to hear your poem."

Morgan handed the lazy lap dog to her dad. Teacup crawled up onto his shoulder, nestled around his neck, and continued to doze.

Morgan stood before her parents, cleared her throat, and giggled.

# A Promise to Teacup

by

Morgan

I wanted a puppy, yes did I
A puppy with its soft little ways
I wanted a puppy, must not tell a lie
Whose time was measured in days

Puppies grow big, they grow and they grow
But that didn't matter to me
That's what I wanted but my dad said "no"
So a puppy was not meant to be

We went to the shelter looking to find
A dog that was already grown
She lay in a cage left there by a lady
Left there by a lady unknown

There sat a doggy so tiny and scared
So lonely and sad, incomplete
The sight of this cannot be compared
All I could hear was my heartbeat

We brought the dog home and I made a promise
The lady who left her could rest
Your dog is with me now, kiss after kiss
I will always give her my best

Morgan's parents delighted in her insightful poem. They commented on how accurately it voiced the story of the past week's events.

"I especially appreciated your words about the woman who had to leave Teacup at the shelter," commented her mom.

Morgan stood quietly for a moment.

She then said, "I've been wondering about the lady. I did not fully understand the story they told us at the shelter. Why *did* she give up her dog to strangers, Mom?"

"Well, sometimes in life we have to make extremely painful decisions that, at the time, are best for everyone. I don't know all the details leading up to that unbearable moment, but I believe it was probably one of the most heartbreaking days of her life."

"Maybe she had no other choice," added her father.

"When we go back to the shelter, perhaps we can inquire about her and uncover the rest of the story," Morgan's mother hoped.

## 4

# *Finding Harriet*

The weekend finally arrived. The family returned to the shelter with Teacup for the evaluation. While her parents talked with the volunteer and the Director of the shelter, Morgan waited out in the lobby. She passed the time by counting the brown paw prints painted on the lobby walls. She tried not to worry.

Morgan cuddled the sleeping dog in her arms. Everyone noticed Morgan's devotion to Teacup. On top of that, Morgan's father showed her poem to the Director. Morgan could see into the office through the glass. The Director seemed impressed. The volunteer also voiced her approval. The Director stamped some papers and then congratulated her parents with a handshake. The volunteer gave Morgan a wink through the window.

She then came out and gave the deserving girl the good news. The wait was finally over. The agony ended. Morgan closed her eyes and smiled as she breathed out a deep sigh of relief. She passed the final test …Teacup could now go home with Morgan forever.

On the drive home, Morgan's father said, "I found out the name of the lady who surrendered Teacup to the shelter. Apparently, the woman's failing health forced her to give up the dog. She could no longer take care of Teacup. I will test out my detective skills and see what I can discover about this mystery woman."

"Dad, what are we going to do, once we figure out who she is?"

"Well, honey, don't you think she would like to know that her beloved Teacup is safe and protected in a loving home?"

"I guess so," Morgan reluctantly responded.

Morgan's mother added, "Wouldn't it be wonderful if we found the 'mystery lady' and took Teacup for a visit? Remember the final verse of your poem, the part about the lady finding peace? *You* could be the one to give her that gift ... the miracle of seeing her precious pet again. Can you even imagine how worried she must be about the dog she raised for ten years? We would be relieving this woman of much pain and sorrow. At this stage in her life, there could be no greater gift. She would truly find peace knowing her dog lives with someone like you."

"I never thought of it that way, Mom. I guess Teacup would like to see her too. Now I can hardly wait! When can we find her, Dad?"

"I will look into it tomorrow."

"What is her name?" asked Morgan's mother.

"Her name is Harriet," said her dad. "I recognized the last name too. She is a retired schoolteacher. I vaguely remember her from my school days. It shouldn't be too difficult to find her."

The following day, when Morgan returned home from school, she found her dad in his study. He was on the phone, making inquiries about Harriet, trying to gather enough information to start his search. He found a possible phone number and address for Harriet.

Later, Morgan's mother called the phone number. It rang and rang; no answer any time of day or night. She tried calling for days.

On the weekend, Morgan's father drove out and found Harriet's house. It was vacant. The lawn was no longer green. A "For Sale" sign flapped in the breeze. He decided to ask around the neighborhood.

He crossed the lawn and rang the doorbell at the house next door. He introduced himself to the people who lived there and informed them of his mission to find Harriet. The friendly couple welcomed him into their home.

Morgan's dad explained about the adoption and his plan to reunite Harriet with her pet. The older couple

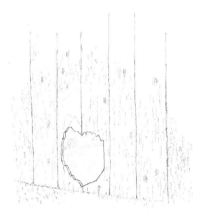

expressed great excitement at the prospect of such a meeting.

They were relieved to hear about the fate of Teacup. They told Morgan's father that the petite poodle often slipped into their yard through an opening in the fence (a hole they purposefully never fixed). She would sneak over almost every day and Harriet had to come looking for her.

The couple laughed and remembered, "Teacup would steal socks, carry them back and forth through the fence, and then hide them in each house. My wife and I appropriately nicknamed her the 'time waster' because we had to go on weekly searches for the missing socks!"

They mentioned that Harriet brought the darling puppy home almost eleven years ago, at a time when they all needed something to brighten their lives. They told Morgan's father that in a way, they too had lost a pet. To their surprise, the retired couple had returned home from an extended cross-country road trip of the National Parks, only to find Harriet and Teacup gone.

The older man shook his head and sighed, "The neighborhood just isn't the same without them. We miss Harriet, and we miss the funny little dog who gave us constant joy."

Morgan's father asked where Harriet lived now. They told him what he needed to know.

# 5

# *Teacup's New Friends*

The worried expression on Teacup's face gradually began to fade. Day by day, she grew more comfortable with her new family. Although, on rare occasions, that "far away" look reappeared. Teacup seemed temporarily lost and confused all over again. When this happened, Morgan just wrapped Teacup in the pink flannel and carried her everywhere, safely scrunched down in the old camera bag until these moments passed.

At bedtime, Teacup hopped all over the bed before settling down. It delighted Morgan to watch this ritual hop every evening. After this comical display, Morgan lifted the top sheet and the tiny animal disappeared

27

under the covers into her cocoon for the night.

On one occasion, Morgan's mother carried the dog to their bedroom to stay overnight. Teacup danced the ritual hop all over their bed too, but refused to crawl under the covers. Instead, she wandered to the edge of the bed and stared down the hallway, towards Morgan's room. After a few minutes of coaxing, her dad willingly admitted defeat and delivered the dog back to Morgan. As the girl slept peacefully, her loyal canine companion slid quietly under the sheet, curled up next to her, and immediately fell asleep.

As she had promised her parents in the beginning, Morgan assumed full responsibility for her pet. She held herself to that promise because she knew her parents expected nothing less.

Morgan loved playing outside with Teacup. It was amazing to see the tiny dog run through the grass.

Compared to the first day, when she would not even take a step, she now claimed the yard with confidence and speed. Sometimes she raced fast enough to make her long, shaggy ears fly straight back, like two silver flags against high winds. At other times, she looked like a giant grasshopper, popping up and down out of the grass, as if her paws were attached to springs. When she got tired, she plopped down, collapsing out of sight in the tall grass. After a short rest, Teacup bravely started all over again—stalking, pouncing, and chasing after Morgan.

Teacup also loved to ride in the wheelbarrow. Morgan

wheeled her around with Teacup's front paws right on the edge, snout forward, as if she were a lookout on the bow of a ship.

One day, it rained. Teacup refused to go outside. Morgan remembered the yellow raincoat that came with the dog. She dressed Teacup in the tiny rubber coat. Properly waterproofed from the weather, the spoiled Teacup trotted willingly out into the rain. She loved rainy days if protected by her raincoat.

However, the raincoat hid any evidence of a dog beneath. The hooded coat draped over her body almost to the ground, showing only the tip of her shiny black nose. When Morgan walked Teacup in the rain, it looked as if she were walking beside a floating yellow raincoat at the end of the leash, instead of a dog. This funny sight caused people to stop and look, pointing and smiling. Teacup was a main attraction whenever she paraded about under her shiny yellow raincoat.

Teacup's cute personality made her a celebrity with the neighbors, especially the two retired sisters who lived down the street. In fact, Morgan met them because of Teacup. When she walked Teacup on the leash, the ladies rarely let her pass without coming out to see the beautiful dog. Morgan visited their house frequently to share priceless moments of her miracle pet.

One of the sisters knitted a pale pink sweater for the canine princess. One day, Morgan dressed Teacup in an angel costume with wings and a halo, showing off a sneak preview of Teacup's next Halloween.

The kind sisters always served tea and treats when Morgan and Teacup visited. It amused them to call these visits—Morgan's "teacup" parties.

Not all of Teacup's new friends were human. Perched high on the fence, far above her reach, sat a cat named Freckles. At first, Teacup would go into attack mode when she saw the towering cat. It was her mission to protect her new kingdom, and there was no place in her kingdom for cats.

Freckles was three times the size of Teacup and famous in the neighborhood for his ability to appear out of nowhere. The magical cat would rush forward unexpectedly, make contact by brushing up swiftly and gently, then disappear as quickly as he came. He repeated this continually throughout the neighborhood, mostly to people. Everyone loved Freckles because he was so entertaining with this magic trick.

One day, Freckles decided to rush Teacup. He appeared without warning, swept by and barely grazed the dog, twirling her slightly off balance. He then vanished like a whirlwind, there one minute and gone the next. Teacup was stunned. Morgan's mother chuckled as she watched the entire comedy from the kitchen window.

Freckles repeated this stunt often. Teacup learned to expect these surprise visits from Freckles. The unsolved mystery of Freckles continued to baffle everyone. No one ever figured out his hiding places, or when he would next materialize. Teacup never knew exactly when or where either, but she sure had fun sniffing the air for Freckles, waiting "on point" for his return.

❖ ❖ ❖

One of Teacup's favorite people was a man named Poppy. Morgan's dad and Poppy were the best of friends. In the beginning, when Poppy came to the house to help her dad with a project, he pretended to overlook the tiny dog. For some curious reason, Teacup always wagged furiously when she saw him. In fact, for everyone else Teacup wagged her tail, but for Poppy, her whole body wagged.

She loved Poppy from the very first meeting. She followed him everywhere, whining at his heels. He could not ignore the wiggly dog for long. He soon fell in love with Teacup, just like everyone else. Now, when he came to visit, he always scooped her up and carried her around possessively.

Whenever Poppy arrived, Morgan revved up the dog, using her most excited voice, "Here comes Uncle Poppy! Here comes Uncle Poppy!"

The dog would always go wild, screeching her deafening high-pitched bark. She dashed as fast as her teeny paws could carry her, lifting off like a flying furball, yelping airborne straight into his arms. Once there, her whole world consisted of nothing else but Poppy. She always nuzzled up closely to him. He kissed the side of her face and talked into her ear. She loved it when Uncle Poppy talked into her ear.

"Such a pretty girl, what a good girl you are, such a pretty girl, yes, a pretty girl you are." She would freeze in place, listening intently, as if his words were whispered secrets containing news of great importance. She would stare sideways at him, showing the whites of her eyes, then suddenly burst into motion, returning his affection by smothering him with kisses of her own.

Poppy built a perch for Teacup to sit in the front window—to watch for Morgan each day. It was equipped with carpeted stairs so she could make her way to the top.

The bond between Teacup and Poppy was particularly special and oddly surprising. Morgan's father always teased his friend about it.

Then, one day, he figured it out. It was something from Teacup's past. He could now see the resemblance ... he believed Poppy reminded Teacup of the man next door in Harriet's old neighborhood.

Mary C. Whitton

# 6
# *The Reunion*

Morgan and her parents drove in silence to the retirement home, the place where Harriet lived. Morgan sat in the back seat, cuddling Teacup on her lap. Many weeks had passed since Harriet had surrendered her precious dog to the shelter.

Morgan tried to imagine what words she would say.

With every step, Morgan drew closer to meeting the phantom woman who had been only a picture in her mind. Just moments away, she was about to come face to face with the person who, without knowing, had given her a priceless gift.

Thinking back now, Morgan suddenly understood how much her life had forever changed, just because she chose that particular day to visit the animal shelter. Just one day later … might have made all the difference in the world.

She followed her parents into the spacious lobby.

A friendly nurse greeted them and led the family down a long hallway, to Harriet's room.

The lady in the bed lay very still. She looked tired and empty, like someone who did not care anymore. Her eyes were open, but they really weren't looking anywhere. Hopelessness was slowly dimming the light from her life. Morgan felt uneasy. Harriet's wrinkled hands were folded on top of the covers. Her body was thin and bent. The room was bare. The plant in the corner did not look real and the TV was unplugged. On the nightstand next to the bed sat two wood-framed photographs. One frame contained a vintage picture of Harriet in her youth, and the other ... a color photograph of Teacup.

The nurse mentioned how Harriet had but a few visitors and seldom came out of her room. She rarely spoke to anyone. She had no family. The nurse touched Harriet's hands and gently woke her from a daydream. The distant longing left her eyes. She responded with a faint yawn.

The nurse spoke in a kind tone.

"Miss Harriet, you have visitors. These people have come to see *you*. They want to speak to you about something important."

"Oh?" said Harriet curiously.

The nurse helped her to sit up, and leaned her back onto the fluffy white pillows. The nurse excused herself, then left the room.

Morgan and her family stood by the bed in a momentary silence.

Harriet's face was kind and pleasant. She turned her head slightly and looked at the group before her.

She just focused on Morgan's mother and asked, "Do I know you, dear?"

"No, Miss Harriet," answered Morgan's mother. "We have never met before today."

Before Harriet could say anything else, Morgan's mother moved in closer. She proceeded to explain to the puzzled lady about the purpose of their visit.

"We are the family who rescued your little dog from the shelter."

Morgan's mom paused, and then repeated more clearly, "We adopted your poodle from the shelter. We figured out how to find you and have brought your Teacup here to see you."

The lady remained bewildered.

Morgan's father motioned to his daughter. Morgan stepped forward, clutching Teacup in her arms.

They could tell that Harriet did not yet understand. They waited for her to absorb the moment.

Slowly, she lowered her eyes to the child before her. She gazed directly into Morgan's eyes for what seemed to be an intensely long time. She then, as if in a trance, looked into Morgan's arms and saw her beloved dog. The disbelief left her speechless. It took Harriet a few seconds to piece it all together. Just then, a look of astonishment dawned on her face. She now understood. Tears immediately filled her formerly vacant eyes.

She whispered emotionally, "TC, oh God in heaven, my precious TC. How did you ... how is this possible?"

Morgan reached across and placed the dog on Harriet's lap. Harriet picked her up. She started to cry happy tears.

"TC, oh TC!" she cried. "Oh TC!"

Teacup also started to remember. She began to wag like a wind-up toy. Teacup showered Harriet with kisses. Harriet could not let her go. The dog, once lost to her forever, was somehow miraculously back in her arms. She held her tightly.

Everyone was smiling and crying at the same time, including the nurses, who came in to see what was happening. It pleased Morgan to have brought joy to such a sad place. This remarkable moment changed Morgan forever, for it was a slice of life at its best.

Morgan and her parents sat down and talked with Harriet for some time. While they chatted, the faithful dog curled up on Harriet's lap as if time had never separated them.

Morgan and Harriet compared stories about Teacup. Morgan learned about Teacup's history, and how it came to be that Harriet assigned her the nickname, "TC."

Morgan's dad spoke of the helpful couple who lived next door to Harriet in the old neighborhood.

"They directed us here. Otherwise, we may have never found you."

Harriet nodded with a grateful smile. Now a twinkle ever present in her eyes.

She told more stories of the people next door.

"We lived on the cliffs overlooking the ocean at Sandy Cove. When I was a little younger, we walked TC down to the beach very carefully on the old wooden stairs. We all loved to watch TC run on the sand. She ran so fast, like a bullet back and forth between us. My loyal friends continued the trek to the shore alone with TC, after it became too difficult for me to descend the steep cliff."

"When they visit me here, we always remember TC and her funny little ways. They were always such wonderful neighbors to me. TC actually thought both homes were her private kingdom, a kingdom she freely roamed! Sometimes she spent as much time next door as she did at my house. They took her in as their own."

She gave a soft chuckle and remembered the regal dog prancing off with a sock and an attitude over to the house next door.

"Teacup was a little sock thief! She trotted so fast and stiffly upright, so proud to have successfully stolen another fallen sock! If we were not careful, off she would sneak, secretly escaping with our socks through a small, heart-shaped hole in the fence."

Harriet said to Morgan, "Give Teacup a sock when you

get home, then watch what happens. She will put on a show guaranteed to bring a laugh. Be careful, though. She'll steal them right out of your closet or from the laundry or right off your foot if you let her!

She smartly uses her paws and teeth to fold the sock over three times to fit in her mouth. Then, she takes off so fast so no one can catch her. She wants you to chase her. Then, once the chase is over, TC will jump onto the bed with her champion head held high, tail wagging, puffed up like royalty, strutting on her victory walk. The only way you will get your sock back is when *she* drops it. If you try to get it back before she is ready, she will give you a stubborn game of Tug-of-War and sound her fake little growl."

Morgan loved hearing the stories of her new dog. She listened and laughed, trying to picture Teacup's past. *Now Morgan knew why fetching a ball or a stick meant nothing to the dainty little dog. What she really wanted was a sock!*

Morgan told Harriet some more recent stories. They all laughed at the antics of the entertaining poodle.

Morgan then asked, "Would you like to hear the poem I wrote about you and Teacup?"

"You wrote a poem? About me?"

"Yes, but I really didn't know you then. So it was

mostly about Teacup and a mystery lady," said Morgan.

She read the poem aloud. Harriet listened to every endearing word. So touched by its sentiment, she asked Morgan's father to pin the handwritten copy on the wall where she could see it.

When it came time to leave, Harriet quietly shed a few more tears of happiness and perhaps loneliness. Today was a good day. In an otherwise bleak existence, today's unexpected visitors charged the room with much emotion and joy.

She knew it was time to return Teacup. She was so delighted and comforted to learn the fate of her precious dog. It was the *not knowing* which haunted her. She could see, with her own eyes, her "TC" was safe and happy with Morgan.

Morgan vowed to visit regularly. She told Harriet they could both be "mommy" to Teacup. Harriet smiled at the sweetness of such an offer and accepted it gladly.

Empty and alone only hours before ... now Harriet, who had nearly given up on living, had gained a new friendship with this nice family. The unhappiness and sorrow that dominated her present-day life faded into a quiet memory.

As for Morgan, she witnessed another person's grief turn into hope. *She truly was the one who brought a cure to the failing spirit of another.*

Morgan and her family visited Harriet's home often.
In fact, Morgan became a regular volunteer. She would
take her miracle dog on rounds throughout the retirement
home and visit the other residents.

Harriet now came out of her room more frequently.
She sometimes walked around with Morgan to share
the cute dog, carrying TC around in the old camera bag.
Morgan noticed how Harriet laughed more and loved to
tell stories about her adventures.

*Many lives changed because of one small dog. Teacup
was not the only one rescued that day at the shelter.
Teacup rescued Morgan too, and together they rescued
Harriet.*

Harriet lived for almost one more year. The last year
and the final days of her life were not spent alone. She
had a family after all. Harriet thanked Morgan and
her parents for their friendship and kindness, and for
bringing TC back to her. She found a final peace knowing
Teacup lived with such a loving family.

A few days after Harriet passed away, her friends
gathered to remember her life. Iris and Elliott, Harriet's
loyal friends from the old neighborhood, were there.
Elliott sang one of Harriet's favorite songs, "Beautiful

Dreamer." His glorious and powerful voice filled the room in her honor.

A few people spoke at the gathering, including Morgan's father. Lora, the volunteer from the shelter, and Uncle Poppy also attended the service. Even some of her students (all grown up now) arrived to celebrate the memory of Harriet. That day, Morgan discovered how one life touches so many others.

Morgan remained quiet on the ride home. She mourned over the loss of Harriet. It made her think. Now, she thought only of Teacup waiting at home for her to return. She reflected back on the day when she adopted Harriet's little dog over a year ago.

Tears came to her eyes as she said in a sniffling voice, "Teacup is almost twelve years old now. Lora, the volunteer, warned me about her age. I can remember the exact words. Do you remember, Mom?"

Morgan paused as she recalled the honest words spoken that day at the shelter.

"Only a few years left to live..." Morgan echoed softly.

Morgan's mother did not respond right away. Instead, she just stared ahead at the road before her.

She then answered her grieving daughter.

"We will be heartbroken just like we are now about Harriet. We will have no choice but to endure the sadness. The grief stays with you in your heart, along with the love. It will be the same with Teacup. She is a cherished member of our family, and losing her will be a deep sorrow."

"It is important to enjoy and savor every moment with Teacup now. This is why you write in your dog journal each day and keep a scrapbook of her precious moments. Do you remember when we adopted Teacup, what else Lora asked you not to forget?"

"Yes, I remember," responded Morgan.

"Lora said pets are like angels. They stay in our lives for only a short time, but they leave wonderful memories and are never forgotten."

"That's right, honey. She also said you never really escape the pain of your loss, but it does soften over time. However brief your time with Teacup will be, it will be worth all the joy and riches she brings to your life. And you will always remember how much you loved her in return.

So, when the time comes to say goodbye, you cling to those memories. Your heart becomes like a magic treasure box of your own unique and special moments. You will be the keeper of her story, and through you, others will remember Teacup. That, in itself, will be your tribute to her. It gives meaning to her existence. Her passing will never wipe away the essence of who she was … and what she meant to us while she lived. As long as you keep the splendor of Teacup alive in your thoughts and dreams, her spirit will live forever."

Morgan understood. She learned, for the first time, how to keep and hold close the memory of a loved one.

"So today we honor Harriet with tears *and* joy, Mom?"

"Yes, Morgan, with tears and joy," repeated her mom sincerely.

"We *celebrate* her life. We continue to do our rounds at her retirement home, sharing Teacup with the other residents. Harriet would be pleased. Harriet would *want* us to laugh ... laugh every time Teacup runs like a bullet, or tosses that silly rabbit with the missing eye and the half-chewed ear, or the way she rides in Grandpa's old wheelbarrow as if she owns the world."

"And most of all!" chimed Morgan, "Harriet would want us to laugh every time Teacup steals another sock!"

Both Morgan and her mother started to laugh through their tears at such an image.

Morgan and her parents shared more funny stories of Teacup, chuckling as they drove towards home.

Morgan could not wait to see Teacup. She remembered a promise she made, in a poem she wrote over a year ago. *Kiss after kiss I will always give her my best.* Morgan felt at peace. She would not trade, for anything in the world, her time together with Teacup ... not even one minute.

"So many lives changed because of you, Morgan," declared her dad.

"Because of *me*?" wondered Morgan.

"Yes, Morgs, it was *you* who stepped up to rescue Teacup at the shelter. You had the courage to take a chance on her. You followed your heart without question. And ever since that day, a miracle has deeply blessed our lives ... the greatest one of all ... the miracle of Love."

When they pulled up into the driveway, Teacup was sitting in the window, waiting for Morgan with a folded sock, ready for a chase. Morgan was happy. She ran in, picked up her sweet little dog and hugged her. She kissed the side of her face and said tenderly, "TC, oh TC."

# THE END

TC AFTER AN EXHAUSTING DAY OF
SOCK THIEVERY

# Morgan's Vocabulary List
## Dictionary

**absorb** – To take in information; to soak in

**adapt** – To change for a reason; to become used to something; adjust

**alter** – To make different in some way; change

**antics** – Funny actions

**anxious** – Worried about the future; uneasy

**astonishment** – Great surprise or amazement

**audible** – To be heard

**baffle** – Confuse

**beneath** – Under; below

**bewildered** – Confused

**bleak** – Gloomy; depressing

**canine** – An animal of the dog family; dogs, wolves, and coyotes

**cherished** – Loved; treasured; appreciated

**comical** – Funny; amusing

**complied** – To comply is to follow the rules; obey

**consume** – To take all of your attention; use up

**content** – Comfortable; happy

**cowering** – Curled up scared; shrink back in fear

**dawned** – To begin to understand something

**descend** – To move downward

**destiny** – Already decided events that happen in one's life beyond our power or control

**determined** – To keep trying; not giving up; fully committed

**devotion** – A feeling of strong love or loyalty

**distinction** – Being able to tell things apart; separate from one another; not alike

**domain** – Region; area; home

**dominate** – To have control or power over something or someone

**elderly** – To be older; approaching old age

**endure** – To carry on through hardships and pain

**evaluation** – To decide the value of something or someone

**existence** – To be alive; to exist; a state of being

**faint** – Not strong; weak

**fate** – A power that decides what will happen; a final outcome

**festive** – Happy; joyous

**foster** – To take care of someone; to act like a parent

**fragile** – Very easy to break or hurt; delicate

**furiously** – Energetically; very active or fast

**grieving** – Suffering over the loss of someone

**huddled** – Standing closely together

**inexperienced** – Having no knowledge or skill that comes from practice

**insightful** – To understand the true nature of something

**instinctively** – To have a feeling inside; to know from within

**intensely** – Extremely strong; to feel deeply

**intently** – Showing great attention and focus; firmly fixed

**liberate** – To set free

**materialize** – To take shape after being invisible; appear

**metallic** – Made of metal; the harsh sound of metal doors closing

**miniature** – A very small copy or model of something; reduced in size

**motionless** – Not moving

**muffled** – Sounds that are not so clear

**oblivious** – Having no clue; unaware

**obvious** – Easily understood

**particularly** – Having to do with one person or thing; special; unusual

**peer** – To look closely into something

**pending** – Not yet decided

**perch** – A high place to sit or roost; like a tree branch for a bird to sit

**persistent** – Refusing to give up or let go

**petite** – Having a small and thin body; tiny; small boned

**phantom** – An image that appears only in the mind; unreal; ghostlike

**pitch** – A certain sound or tone

**ponder** – To think about something deeply and carefully

**possessively** – Having a strong desire to own something or someone

**prospect** – The idea of something that will happen

**purposefully** – To have a goal; aim; intention

**realization** – To understand something; to see the truth

**regal** – Belonging to a king or queen; royal

**remarkable** – Worthy of being noticed; uncommon; exceptional

**resemblance** – Looking like someone else

**ritual** – Routine ceremony; habit

**savor** – To enjoy the value of something; appreciate

**sentiment** – Feeling; emotion

**spacious** – Large; roomy

**splendor** – Full of wonder; brilliance

**strutting** – Showing off; to walk in a proud manner

**surrendered** – To give up something to the control of another

**suspended** – To cause to stop for a period of time; to hang from a higher position

**sympathetic** – Feeling or showing understanding to someone who is suffering

**temporarily** – Not forever; for a limited time

**threshold** – The piece of wood, metal, or stone that forms the bottom of a doorway

**tilting** – One side that is higher than the other; to lean to one side

**timid** – Shy

**topic** – Something or someone people write about; subject of conversation; theme

**torture** – Great pain; suffering

**trek** – To make a slow and difficult journey; to make one's way slowly

**tribute** – Mark of respect or praise; compliment

**unbearable** – unable to endure the pain; too difficult to accept

**unexpectedly** – Suddenly; surprisingly; coming without warning

**unique** – Being the only one of its type; different from everything else

**vacant** – Empty

**vague** – Not clear in meaning; difficult to remember

**vintage** – A well-made item from the past; old-fashioned

TC ON A RAINY DAY

THE AUTHOR WITH TC

THE REAL HARRIET

THE REAL UNCLE POPPY – BILL CAUSLEY

ANIMAL LOVER AND ADVOCATE – LORA THILL

FRECKLES AND HER
FAMILY MEMBER –
EVYN WHITTON

THE REAL PEOPLE NEXT DOOR
IRIS AND ELLIOTT WHITTON

ELLIOTT WHITTON

IRIS AND OUR BELOVED TC

More About the Author

**Performed** (singing) in venues throughout Europe with *I Cantori di Carmel*:
St. Andra Church - Salzburg, Austria
St. Petrus Canisius Church - Vienna, Austria
Basilica Santa Maria Gloriosa dei Frari - Venice, Italy
Basilica di San Antonio, Padova, Italy
Duomo - Cathedral de St. Maria del Fiore - Florence, Italy
St. George Church- Innsbruck, Austria
St. Florian's Monastery - Austria
Strasbourg Cathedral - Strasbourg, France
St. Matthias Church - Budapest, Hungary
Oskar Nedbal Theater - Tabor, Czech Republic
The Mirror Chapel of the National Library - Prague, Czech Republic
Officers Club, U.S. 1st Infantry Division -Bamberg, Germany
St Martins Church - Bamberg, Germany
Eglise Sacre Coeur - Howald, Luxembourg
Notre Dame Cathedral - Paris, France
Chartres Cathedral - Chartres, France

**Toured:**
St. Thomas Church - Strasbourg, France
where Albert Schweitzer played the grand Pipe Organ in 1908
(Miss Mary's personal idol)
The Mozart Birth Museum - Salzburg, Austria
Schonbrunn Palace – Vienna, Austria
Vienna State Opera House – Vienna, Austria
Gondola through canals of Venice, Italy
Accademia Gallery (Michelangolo's Statue of David) – Florence, Italy
Louvres (Leonardo da Vinci's Mona Lisa) – Paris, France
Slovenian Philharmonic Concert Hall (where Beethoven
conducted the first performance of his "Pastoral Symphony")
Lucerne and Liechtenstein, Switzerland
Train ride from Grindelwald to Kleine Scheidegg through
the Alps – Switzerland
The American Battle Monuments and Memorial which includes
the burial site of General George S. Patton – Luxemboug
Jewish Quarter – Prague, Czech Republic

## Boronda Music Scholarship:
Mexico City
Toured many cities of Mexico
Sent to the Yucatan Peninsula
Toured the Mayan Archeological sites
Traveled to Teotihuacan, Mexico
Climbed to the top of the Pyramid of the Sun - the third largest
pyramid in the world
Climbed to the top of the Pyramid of the Moon

## Travels to Africa:
Nairobi National Museum - Nairobi, Kenya
Nyeri, Kenya.  Toured home of Lord Baden-Powell,
(Founder of the Boy Scouts)
Stayed in the famous Treetops Hotel to view animals from balcony
Mt. Kenya Safari Club Game Reserve Safari
Nairobi - Aberdare National Park Safari
Crossed the Equator to Samburu Game Reserve Safari
Masai Mara Game Reserve Safari
Hot-Air Ballooned over the Serengeti in the Masai Mara, viewed the
animals from above, including the Great Migration
Mombasa Island, Kenya.  Boating on Indian Ocean


## Travels in US:
Grand Canyon
Zion National Park
Bryce Canyon
Sedona
Yellowstone
The Grand Tetons
Yosemite
Death Valley
Catalina
Boated Down the Snake River
Boated Down the Rogue River
Puerto Rico

54588281R00044